INSPIRATION
IN THE

INSPIRATION
IN THE

A JOURNAL FOR EXPLORING *Life*

Yvette McQueen, MD

INSPIRATION IN THE CLOUDS

Published by Purposely Created Publishing Group™

Copyright © 2020 Yvette McQueen

All rights reserved.

No part of this book may be reproduced, distributed or transmitted in any form by any means, graphic, electronic, or mechanical, including photocopy, recording, taping, or by any information storage or retrieval system, without permission in writing from the publisher, except in the case of reprints in the context of reviews, quotes, or references.

Printed in the United States of America

ISBN: 978-1-64484-211-9

Photo Credit: Yvette McQueen, MD

Special discounts are available on bulk quantity purchases by book clubs, associations and special interest groups. For details email: sales@publishyourgift.com or call (888) 949-6228.

For information log on to www.PublishYourGift.com

This journal belongs to

―――――――――――――――――――――――――

"Every great dream begins with a dreamer.
Always remember, you have within you the strength,
the patience, and the passion to reach for the stars
to change the world."

—Harriet Tubman

A cloud is a visible mass of condensed water vapor floating at different levels in the atmosphere, typically high above the ground. I fly several times a month and always feel an exhilaration when the airplane passes through the clouds. Clouds may look like cotton balls, but they are not solid structures. They can be fluffy, thin and sparse, and even scary at times. And even though the pattern of clouds is random, and scientifically, I know I can fall right through them, clouds make me feel safe, as if they are ready to give me a big hug. The variability of the patterns and shapes of the clouds inspires my thoughts.

The purpose of this journal is for you to enjoy the view within the clouds and gain inspiration from some familiar quotations. Clear your thinking, let your mind explore, and write down your inspiring thoughts about life.

Live Well,
Yvette McQueen, MD
A Global Traveling Physician

"Act as if what you do makes a difference. It does."

—William James

"Never bend your head. Always hold it high. Look the world straight in the eye."

—Helen Keller

___
___
___
___
___
___
___
___
___
___
___
___
___
___
___

"Believe you can and you're halfway there."

—Theodore Roosevelt

"You are never too old to set another goal or to dream a new dream."

—C. S. Lewis

"Sometimes you will never know the value of a moment until it becomes a memory."

—Dr. Seuss

"The purpose of life is to live it, to taste experience to the utmost, to reach out eagerly and without fear for newer and richer experience."

—Eleanor Roosevelt

"If I cannot do great things, I can do small things in a great way."

—Martin Luther King Jr.

"Strive not to be a success, but to be of value."

—Albert Einstein

"Keep your face towards the sunshine and the shadows will fall behind you."

—Walt Whitman

"When everything seems to be going against you, remember that the airplane takes off against the wind, not with it."

—Henry Ford

"Peace begins with a smile."

—Mother Teresa

"It always seems impossible until it's done."

—Nelson Mandela

"What lies behind you and what lies in front of you pales in comparison to what lies inside of you."

—Ralph Waldo Emerson

"Life is 10% what happens to you and 90% how you react to it."

—Charles R. Swindoll

"Don't let yesterday take up too much of today."

—Will Rogers

Life is not always sunshine and blue skies. Adversity will either break you or make you stronger. Surround yourself with people who will hold you, or have lots of glue.

"Adopt the pace of nature: her secret is patience."

—Ralph Waldo Emerson

"Learn from yesterday, live for today, hope for tomorrow. The important thing is not to stop questioning."

—Albert Einstein

"It's not what you look at that matters,
it's what you see."

—Henry David Thoreau

When you break through those low-lying clouds, keep climbing. The dream is within sight.

"My mission in life is not merely to survive, but to thrive; and to do so with some passion, some compassion, some humor, and some style."

—Maya Angelou

"Believe in yourself! Have faith in your abilities! Without a humble but reasonable confidence in your own powers you cannot be successful or happy."

—Norman Vincent Peale

"Twenty years from now you will be more disappointed by the things that you didn't do than by the ones you did do. Sail away from the safe harbor. Explore. Dream. Discover."

—Mark Twain

"The only person you are destined to become is the person you decide to be."

—Ralph Waldo Emerson

"You yourself, as much as anybody in the entire universe, deserve your love and affection."

—Gautama Buddha

"It is during our darkest moments that we must focus to see the light."

—Aristotle

"Life is like riding a bicycle. To keep your balance you must keep moving."

—Albert Einstein

"No act of kindness, no matter how small,
is ever wasted."

—Aesop

"Success is not final, failure is not fatal: It is the courage to continue that counts."

—Winston Churchill

"With the new day comes new strength and new thoughts."

—Eleanor Roosevelt

Connect with Dr. Yvette!

Visit her website at
www.yvettemcqueenmd.com

Visit her on Facebook, Instagram,
Twitter, and LinkedIn
@yvettemcqueenmd

CREATING DISTINCTIVE BOOKS WITH INTENTIONAL RESULTS

We're a collaborative group of creative masterminds with a mission to produce high-quality books to position you for monumental success in the marketplace.

Our professional team of writers, editors, designers, and marketing strategists work closely together to ensure that every detail of your book is a clear representation of the message in your writing.

Want to know more?
Write to us at info@publishyourgift.com
or call (888) 949-6228

Discover great books, exclusive offers, and more at
www.PublishYourGift.com

Connect with us on social media

@publishyourgift

www.ingramcontent.com/pod-product-compliance
Lightning Source LLC
Chambersburg PA
CBHW040002110526
44587CB00001BA/27